On the Job

Firefighters
In Our Community

Michelle Ames

PowerKiDS press™

New York

To Papa John

Published in 2010 by The Rosen Publishing Group, Inc.
29 East 21st Street, New York, NY 10010

First Edition

Editor: Nicole Pristash
Book Design: Greg Tucker
Photo Researcher: Jessica Gerweck

Photo Credits: Cover ML Harris/Getty Images; p. 5 © www.iStockphoto.com/Shaun Lowe; pp. 7, 9, 13, 17, 24 (left), 24 (left-center) , 24 (right) Shutterstock.com; pp. 11, 21 Code Red/Getty Images; pp. 15, 24 (right-center) © www.iStockphoto.com/Jason Martin; p. 19 Getty Images.

Library of Congress Cataloging-in-Publication Data

Ames, Michelle.
  Firefighters in our community / Michelle Ames. — 1st ed.
      p. cm. — (On the job)
  Includes index.
  ISBN 978-1-4042-8058-8 (library binding) — ISBN 978-1-4358-2455-3 (pbk.) —
ISBN 978-1-4358-2463-8 (6-pack)
  1. Fire extinction—Juvenile literature. 2. Fire fighters—Juvenile literature. I. Title.
  TH9148.A48 2010
  628.9'25—dc22

2008049033

Manufactured in the United States of America

Contents

A firefighter's job is to put out fires.

Firefighters ride in fire trucks.
Fire trucks move quickly.

If there is a fire in a tall building, a firefighter climbs a **ladder** to reach the fire.

Sometimes, firefighters have to stand in a **bucket** to get to a fire.

To put a fire out, firefighters **spray** water on it.

A firefighter must wear a **mask** to keep safe from smoke.

Firefighters sometimes put out car fires.

This firefighter is working to stop a wildfire. A wildfire is a forest fire.

Firefighters even use **helicopters** to put out forest fires!

Firefighters work together to keep people safe.

Words to Know

bucket

helicopter

ladder

mask

spray

Index

Web Sites

Due to the changing nature of Internet links, PowerKids Press has developed an online list of Web sites related to the subject of this book. This site is updated regularly. Please use this link to access the list:

www.powerkidslinks.com/job/fire/